# Memories by Mom

## Tales of an
## Alaskan Bush Pilot
## and His Family

"Mom" Giordano and Mary Halpin

Publication Consultants

*PO Box 221974 Anchorage, Alaska 99522-1974*

ISBN 1-888125-71-3


Library of Congress Catalog Card Number: 00-105347


Copyright 2000 by Mary Halpin
—First Edition—


Drawings by "Mom" Giordano
Photographs from the Giordano family collection

Manufactured in the United States of America.

I DEDICATE THIS BOOK to my Dad, who at age 78, is still going strong, and as stubborn as the day is long.

He is well-known in the construction business, as he worked in construction for well over 30 years. He worked on most of the roads in Alaska today—from Homer to Barrow. His crew admired and respected him. They knew when Dad told them what needed to be done, no matter what it was—it was done—no questions asked.

At age 78 he still has a foreman's attitude. He may not be able to do the work, but he sure knows how to give orders. And things are still done his way—no questions asked.

He is full of wit and humor and a bit of the ole' Blarney. No, he isn't Irish, he's Italian. But it's his wit and humor that's kept him rolling along all these years. Hopefully it will keep him going for many more.

As heroes go, I guess you could say he's at the top of my list.

I think when God made Dad, he figured he'd best break the mold. The world couldn't handle two of them!

# Table of Contents

# Introduction

THIS BOOK IS MORE of our memories of growing up in homesteading days. But it will have a few more stories of my Dad's flying experiences as told by him.

I hope I can put his excitement on paper, because to listen, and watch him as he told these stories were the best part of these stories, The way his eyes would light up and twinkle, the hand gestures he made were more part of the stories as the stories themselves.

Of course, there will be more of Mom's and my memories as before, with a few of Mom's recipes she created out of necessity, after all necessity is the mother of invention!! It's called making do with what you have.

So sit back, grab a cup of coffee, and enjoy the humorous side of life as it was in the homesteading days.

# Dad's Pride and Joy

ONE OF DAN'S DREAMS was to have his own plane. One of the fellows he worked for just happened to have a plane for sale.

It was an Aeronica Champ with a 90 horse powered engine. He had started his lessons out at Lake Hood, in Anchorage. But then it was summer, so he was learning to take off and land with wheels.

When it came time to land, with skis, he had hired an instructor to come out to the Willow Airstrip each Sunday until Dad was able to take off and land with skis.

When Sunday arrived, Dad was anxiously waiting at the Willow strip. The instructor never showed. By this time Dad could fly, and take off with wheels—so, tired of waiting—he decides to go up on his own. The take off was fine—after all it wasn't much different from wheels, the skis were on the ground. So up he went, flying around and having a good ole' time.

Now came the time to land, and call it a day. Now considering he had only landed with wheels he figured no problem, piece of cake. To say the least his first landing on skis was a bit rough, and scary for Mom, as she was waiting in the car. He came in at a nice pace, but didn't allow for the fact that he had no wheels— being use to landing with wheels he dropped her down to what he figured would be solid ground. The distance that the wheels would have covered wasn't there!! So down he came, bouncing and skiing down the strip, right towards Mom, who at this time was just hoping he would stop soon.

Yes, he did stop with plenty of distance from Mom, and he was so impressed with his first landing on skis that he never did hire another instructor to teach him how to land on skis.

DAD, MOM, AND MARY

# *Homemakers*

BY THE TIME ALL THE CHILDREN were in school, and the older two were married, I actually had time on my hands. So, I had decided to form a Homemakers Club. Some of the neighbors, plus daughter's-in-laws, now joined Willows first Homemaker Club. The officers read, Giordano, Giordano, Giordano, and Giordano!

Each week one of the members would give a demonstration on her favorite handwork. We held a plant sale and provided food baskets for several needy families at Thanksgiving and Christmas-also collecting items for families who had been burnt out.

One year Dan and I got word of a real needy family too late for our club to take action. Dan an I hastily gathered enough food, toys, and clothing, and went to their home. Upon arriving , we found a note on the door saying, "Come on in, we'll be back shortly." Giggling like to school kids, we piled everything on the table and rushed away before anyone caught us. I wish I had been a fly on the wall, just to see their faces when they came home to a happy Christmas after all.

At that time Willow was small, and definitely out in the sticks, so no one bothered to lock doors.

We had a standing rule in our house to all the community, if they couldn't make it home, either because of bad roads, or you just had a few too many down at the local pub, our doors always open, grab a sleeping bag from the corner and make yourself comfortable, just don't wake up the household. So, many mornings we woke to find someone sleeping on our front room floor.

*"MOM" GIORDANO*

Willow's first grocery store.

# Cranberry Liquor

LIVING IN WILLOW, there was an abundance of berries, Just waiting for picking. Also it helped to increase our food supplies in the winter when Dad wasn't working.

A friend of mine had made a liqueur of cranberries. Another had made cranberry relish to go with meat dishes. I tried the relish first:

> Grind up a gallon of cleaned cranberries along with an apple and an orange. Core your apple, but do not peel the orange, just remove the seeds. Add a cup of sugar, not to much or it will get too juicy. And lose it's flavor. Add a couple tablespoons of lemon juice, mix thoroughly, and place in glass jars for two weeks.

Delicious with meats, and adds a special touch to your meals.

The liqueur you crush several gallons of cranberries, saving as much of the juice as possible. Straining the mass through a strainer, although in the early days we use to use cheese cloth. You let it drain for several days. By now you should have good, clear, juice. Add equal parts of "ever clear" to the juice and you have a nice liqueur.

Dad loved it!!

Rose hip jam was another delightful delicacy. I learned to make for us. I didn't make it to often because the rose-hips had quite a few berries in them and took longer to clean. This was a good source of vitamin c, so I had to try this recipe.

> A couple quarts of cleaned rose-hips, cored and peeled apple. Add a couple cups of or so of sugar, and water, mix until smooth, stirring a couple of times to keep from scorching. Add a box of pectin to make sure it jelled. Place in glass jars to cool. After it cools, cap with melted wax and store until your ready to use.

As I said, it's a good source of vitamin C, but I don't think the kids were fond of it, so I only made it once. It did help out when making lunches- -when we ran out of raspberry jam, it was time for some rose-hip jam!

"MOM" GIORDANO

# Willow P.T.A.

TALKING TO A NEIGHBOR the other day, put me in mind of P.T.A. back in the 60s. She was telling me of a project the P.T.A. was doing and asking some advice.

I had become a member of the Willow P.T.A. in the early 60s and had stayed active in the group for many years, at least all the years I had kids in school.

Many homesteaders came and went. Coming to Alaska was a great opportunity for many families to acquire land. We all had to build habitable dwellings, a refuse pit, (I think more to feed the bears, than disposing of garbage), clear and seed 20 acres of the 160 acre parcel. Sure, it was a rough life, and some women left their men, and some entire families left. So we had a big turnover in students and in P.T.A. members.

One day, as a handful of P.T.A. members gathered, it was suggested we disband. One gentleman said very clearly that their wasn't one person intelligent enough to hold office. I figured he must have been talking about himself. He the abruptly left. Well, I resented that remark so much that I stood up and volunteered to be president. As president I could assign necessary officers to make our P.T.A. function normally, and accomplish some important tasks.

After waiting, and not hearing to much noise, I stood up and started pointing a finger at individuals, stating, "your treasurer, your secretary, and your vice-president". Now we had a real P.T.A. group. Little was done at the first official meeting, the new officers collected as much past records together that they could find, and from that point on, I'm happy to say our meeting went along without a hitch.

Our P.T.A. grew in membership, and we funded many projects for the needs of our school, including playground equipment. We also had a skating rink (we cleared a large section of the lake for the kids) and we provided skates until we had a serious accident and someone got hurt. We funded annual Halloween carnivals, had Thanksgiving dinners, and Christmas dinners, also. And we certainly couldn't forget Valentines day! These event were for the whole community to enjoy, as well as for the students.

The costume party for Halloween, we had a cake walk, ghost house, cider sold by a "real" witch (me) and a costume contest for each grade. And everyone got a bag of goodies as they came in the door—Now, to make the cider look more like a witches brew, we had put it in a huge bucket, added dry ice so it would steam-it sure looked real, of course that's when I found out that putting dry ice in to regular cider, made it Hard cider-so out came another huge kettle, regular ice and regular cider-every one found it funny, and even though we had to get rid of the hard cider, fun was had by all. The women of the community baked cakes for our cake walk, others in the community volunteered to run our game booths, and others were judges for the costume contest. Local businesses donated to defray the costs of prizes and goodies. None the less, fun was had by all.

A dinner was served at Thanksgiving and Christmas. At Christmas we had a tree, and Mr. & Mrs. Santa Clause came, giving gifts to all the children. One year I was asked to be Mrs. Santa Clause, I guess Santa had a cold or something and couldn't make it, anyway, they couldn't find a dress in my size, so they handed me 5 yards of red material and asked if I could make my own dress. Why not, I made outfits all the time for my own children. So I made my dress and trimmed it with real rabbit fur, Dan trapped a lot of them in the winter, after they turned white. Another year I was asked to crochet 2 Christmas stockings, 1 green for the girls, and 1 red for the boys, both were filled with toys and goodies. We then raffled them off at the P.T.A Christmas party. The stockings were requested back for several years. I imagine they wore out, but I don't know for sure of their demise.

But I was delighted that we never gave up on our little P.T.A.

*"MOM" GIORDANO*

# My First Dog Sled Ride

HAVING THE IDITAROD restart in Willow was a big surprise for me. When I told people I lived in Willow, the usual response was, "Where's Willow?" It was generally not on any maps. It is nice now for me to see the maps showing Willow.

In Willow, at first, very few people had dog teams, and those that did, had them for transportation in the winter, not for racing.

My first dog team ride was not really planned. My son and I had walked up Hatcher Pass to visit a friend. She was a good cook, and had invited us for lunch. We had stayed and enjoyed her cooking, and the conversation. Being winter, we knew we had to leave in time to make it back home before dark, as in the winter, darkness fell early—usually about 4 p.m., or so.

As we stepped out her door for our trip home, we spotted a moose down the road. Not wanting to encounter this moose, we asked the next door neighbor for a ride home. He had a truck, but no gas. But he did offer us a ride home with his dog team. Hitching up the team, I was surprised to see the sled. It was an ochio, an army sled. No the usual sled used by dog mushers. By now I was feeling a little bit dubious of this ride home. But between the dog sled ride, or the moose —some choice. We chose the dog sled ride!

His dogs were mixed breeds, and ready for the trip. I cautiously got in the sled. I sat in the middle on blankets, my son knelt behind me. Our neighbor was in the front of the sled, and yelled "Mush!" The dogs obeyed the command, and took off smoothly along until we rounded a corner. Sure enough, there was that moose. She was unwilling to leave the road, as hard, high snow berms lined the sides of the road. The dogs now stepped up their pace, and so did the moose. She ran faster, and faster. The ochio was whipping behind the dogs. My son was told to drag his feet, to act as a brake. The neighbor yelled at his dogs to "whoa." I held on to the sides of the ochio, skinning my knuckles as it whipped side to side. Finally, in fear and desperation the moose jumped over the berm, instantly she disappeared.

The dogs sped on, not even breaking stride. I believe, if you could have clocked this fine team, that they surely must have been doing at least 60 mph! None the less, we did make it home. Catching my breath, and making sure my son was okay., I was barely able to say thank you for the ride home.

Mr. Nelson, another infamous name in the iditarod history, moved out to Willow. He owned the Howling Dog Farm that had started in Anchorage. He invited many other mushers to stay and train at his farm.

Willow now host many mushers who enter the Iditarod. Having the Iditarod restart in willow is a rare occasion. It is only held in Willow when there is a lack of snow in Wasilla.

Four-mile Road, where we lived in Willow, now has at
least four residents that now have dog teams. Most own
over 100 dogs or more. It's easy to tell when it is feeding
time for the dogs. Now if you could imagine the noise
that over 400 dogs could make, howling and barking as
they wait for their meal you'd probably wish you were
like my Dad—deaf as a doornail!

*"MOM" GIORDANO*

# Ole' Crash and Burn

I KNEW DAN FLEW, and had a lot of close calls that he never told anyone about. So whenever he would say, "I'm taking the plane up for awhile." I would always hold my breath and pray for the time he walked back in the door.

This one particular day, he came to say he was going to check his trap line across the Susitna River, and he was taking a neighbor with him. It was a cold winter day, and when they had finished checking the traps they came back to the plane to head home.

Again, being cold and impatient, he started the plane, but didn't allow enough time for the engine to warm. After getting airborne and gaining some space between the plane and the ground, the plane stalled. He made several attempts to get the plane restarted, but to no avail. Now he had to look for a place to put the plane down, without doing too much damage, let alone not getting hurt too bad upon landing. He spotted two trees and aimed for the space between them. The trees sheared off both wings, and the plane landed in a heap between them. Both were shaken, but unhurt. They both climbed out the windows of the plane glad to be alive and not injured. Dan then took the seat out of the plane, and poured gas on it and started a fire to keep them warm, it was to late in the day to try to walk out.

It just so happened that the same day Dan crashed his plane, another pilot had also gone down. So the FAA were out searching for this lost pilot when they came across Dan's wrecked plane. They knew it wasn't who they were looking for, and saw two set of prints heading away from the crash sight.

In the meantime I was home trying to keep my calm, and keep the kids calm and secure that their dad would be home soon. The neighbor wife was also at my house, and very upset. It wasn't easy for me to keep everybody's hopes and spirits up, and control my own feelings under check.

As I was holding the neighbors wife, trying to calm her down, I was just about to loose faith my self, when much to my surprise, I looked up and there was Dan's face in the window.

Everyone was relieved, our neighbors went home, all was well. A few days later we got a visit from the FAA. They came in and told Dan they were investigating he accident. They asked to see his medical card, Dan said he didn't have one, how about a license, they asked. Dan's reply was I don't have one. In the early days, and you took no passengers with you, you didn't need a license.

Now the FAA wanted to know if you didn't have a passenger with you, why were there two sets of prints leading out of the plane. Dan had his explanation ready, and his reply was, "I hit my head, and was a bit dazed, so I must have climbed out one side, lost my sense of direction and made a full circle, climbed back in the plane, and crawled out the other side."

I'm most sure that the FAA didn't believe his story, but they couldn't prove whether that happened or not. So the most they could do was give him a slight slap on the hand and make him get a license to fly.

I was relieved to see him come home from that incident, and secretly glad that he wrecked his plane. I slept a lot easier after that.

*"MOM" GIORDANO*

# *Majestic Mountains*

GROWING UP IN WILLOW, I found two things fascinating.

One was the moose, because of the fact that they are so huge, awkward looking, and gangly. But despite their looks, they could still manage to disappear into the woods so fast, and not even leave a trace!!

The mountains were my second. In the winter, when covered with snow, you could use your imagination and see many pictures on the mountain sides. For instance, when one mountain (I don't know it's name) is covered with snow and then the winds pick up and blow the snow of the ridges, it leaves a resemblance of Cher with her long black hair and high cheek bones. Coming from Anchorage, past the Parks Highway light, driving the Glenn Highway, you'll come to a sign on the right — Central Asphalt and Paving. Looking behind the rock quarry at the mountains behind it, you will see her. Try it some time and see if you can picture her there.

I think my most favorite mountain, though, is Mount Susitna, nicknamed Sleeping Lady.

There is an ancient folklore linked to this mountain. It tells of a woman named Susitna, who belonged to a race of giants. It goes on to tell that her boyfriend left the village to ward off hostile invaders.

While waiting for her boyfriend's return, she laid down and went to sleep. Her boyfriend dies in battle, and the villagers don't want to wake Susitna and tell her the sad news. She's been asleep ever since. Today she is known as Mount Susitna, a mountain that resembles a sleeping lady.

I have always envisioned her as lying on her back, with her arms folded across her chest, and her long hair flowing behind her. Recently, I saw an illustration a woman had done, but she is lying on her side, but her long hair is still flowing behind her.

I have taken many photos of this magnificent mountain, at various times of the day. The one I like the most, was taken at sunset, where she is silhouetted in the sunset. One photo of her that I haven't yet tried taking, is coming across the Knik River Bridge. From that view point you get the wide expanse of the Knik River where it flows into the ocean. In the winter, the river is covered with ice and snow, and on a bright sunny day, it makes a beautiful picture. But I haven't been brave enough yet to stop on the bridge and take her picture.

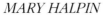

*MARY HALPIN*

# *State Fair*

BEING TYPICAL KIDS, we always looked forward to the fair. For us, it was carnival rides, cotton candy, seeing livestock exhibits, and more cotton candy.

One year my younger brother entered his pet rabbit. At home it was his chore to take care of our two rabbits. We had one female, and one male. Mom always told him to be sure not to let the two in the same cage, never telling him why. And every other day he would go out and clean the cages, feed and water them.

One looked real nice and healthy, and was bigger than the other, so came the idea for him to enter this rabbit in fair.

Mom took us down before the fair, so we could get his rabbit entered, and ready for judging. We could hardly wait to go to the fair and see how his rabbit had done.

The day of the fair, our first priority was to go see the rabbits and find out how his rabbit fared. Were we ever surprised to see a purple ribbon, Grand Champion. With my brother's name on it, hanging off the cage. My brother was so proud, and so were we.

We went about enjoying the rest of the fair. Riding on the rides, eating cotton candy, Mom always brought our lunch with us, as the food in the fair for nine children was a bit expensive. So it was like having a picnic, along with the fair. We always loved going to the fair.

After the fair, we went back to pick my brother's prize rabbit up and bring it home. He went back to cleaning the cages, feeding and watering them as before. A couple of days after the fair, he came running in after cleaning the cages to inform Mom that his prize rabbit (who was suppose to be male) had babies. Mom was shocked to say the least, after all, how could the judges miss the fact that he was a she!! She asked my brother if he had been keeping the rabbits separated, and he replied, "Yes, Mom, except when I cleaned the cages, then I put them in one cage together, while I cleaned the other." Now, we kids didn't object, now there were plenty of rabbits for all, and a few to give away. We had a lot of fun playing with our new pets. We just thought, a rabbits a rabbit, we didn't care about things like what happens when you put a male and female together.

Mom never tried to explain, she just let us enjoy them, but did insist on giving a few away.

*MARY HALPIN*

# *Our First Christmas*

GETTING READY FOR THIS CHRISTMAS Season put me in mind of our first Christmas in Alaska. I had secretly put a small suitcase of Christmas baubles on the truck when we left Massachusetts. I carefully wrapped, and tucked the ornaments between paper, sure all would be safe. When we unloaded the truck I hid the suitcase without opening it. Imagine my dismay when Christmas came and not everything in the suitcase was able to endure the rigors of the Alaskan Highway. All that lay intact was a chocolate Santa that was in David's stocking the year before we left Mass.. Each child had received a one, but David, at 6 months, was unable to eat his.

Well, we all sat down to make home made decorations. The children made chains out of colored pages of a catalog, they also strung popcorn, cut designs from tin can covers, and I made a huge star from a coffee can lid for the top of the tree.

The boys went out and cut down a tree, and brought it in, and we proceeded to decorate it with our meager decorations. To the children, it was a fantastic tree, and they just loved it.

The community also celebrated Christmas together. One year, because of my "ample" form, I was asked to play Mrs. Santa, I made the dress out of material they had supplied, trimmed it with rabbit fur, and I was set. They forgot to tell me that I was to arrive in a dogsled!!

They placed me in the dog sled at the beginning of the community hall's driveway. Santa, a 300 pound neighbor, was on the sled's runners in back. Mr. Mack's dog team of nine dogs hadn't run all winter, and were raring to go. Mr. Mack had his lead dog on a choke chain, and when he said, "Mush," the dogs took off on a dead run. I was hanging on for dear life. The dogs were dragging Mr. Mack on the seat of his pants, and Mr. Santa was hollering, "whoa" to no avail!

Four men stood at the door of the hall, and when the doors opened, they managed to lift the sled over the two steps that led into the hall. The dogs never hesitated—in they went. Dragging me and the sled behind them. I was suppose to say "Merry Christmas" but by then I was too scared that I couldn't' utter a word!! I even remember if I waved either. I was just glad that the dogs had stopped. I still say that if those doors hadn't opened, we'd probably ended up in Talkeetna!! Thank heavens that facing all those children, the dogs did calm down.

*"MOM" GIORDANO*

# Mom's Antiques

MOM WAS MOST DETERMINED to bring all of her antiques with her. Of, course, Dad was just as determined that there wasn't room, and there for not necessary.

As stated before, in other stories, when we arrived in Alaska, and started unloading the truck, Dad was surprised to find her antiques. He also told her that they probably caused the loss of one of the springs on the truck.

But, as time went along, the antiques claimed another category in our lives. They became household items.

The antique washboard was well over 100 years old. When we lived in Massachusetts, Dad worked on demolishing old house. While working on one of these houses, he found the washboard in the wall of this house, and brought it home to Mom. Little did she know at that time, that in the future it would come in very handy. She always said she invented cold water detergent, because it took too long to heat enough water to wash clothes for 11 people. Many a time, as a child, I watched as she washed clothes in the winter, with ice chunks in the water.

She brought about 6 antique kettles, and they also were used to make soups, stews, and roasts in them. She also had about 3 old fashion cast iron, irons, which were well used also. They were the kind you put on the stove, heated until hot enough to use for ironing. Iron free clothing wasn't available then. She even had an old fashion potato masher, and it also became a useful kitchen utensil. The old fashion pill grinder she never found much use for—so it still fell into the category of being an antique.

As years went by, and we became more modernized, these useful items once again claimed the category of antiques. She used the kettles for flower pots out in the yard and the rest took their place on shelves for decoration.

She still has the antique washboard, crock, potato masher, and pill grinder. Over the years she has added an old fashion plunger, made of metal, and an egg-weigher. The kettles got lost in one of their moves, though.

In 1995, when we moved to Palmer, she made a flower garden out of a brass bead, only because we couldn't find her and old fashioned iron bed. But, it is the center of attraction at all of her yard sales, and friendly get togethers.

After making one in the front yard out of a double brass bed, with porcelain, flowered balls, we found her a single brass, bed. So she made another brass garden bed in the back yard, also.

*MARY HALPIN*

# Never Again

DURING THE WINTER, Dad had plenty of time for himself. One of his favorite past times, was to take the plane out for a spin in the early afternoon, as by 4:30 p.m. it was getting dark.

Usually his little spins found him down at the Willow Trading Post, and having a drink or two while he traded stories with other locals.

One fellow was always there, and he would always ask Dad to take him up for a ride in the plane. Dad would reply that he couldn't because he he'd had a couple of drinks, and didn't feel safe in giving him a ride.

One particular day, Dad went down early, had his drinks, and story telling time, when the neighbor came in. The neighbor started again on Dad to take him up for a ride. Dad still insisted that he'd had a couple of drinks and didn't feel safe about taking him for a ride. The neighbor then proceeded to tell Dad that he thought Dad didn't like him, and that's why Dad wouldn't take him up. Dad listened to this for awhile, and finally turned the guy and said, "You want to go up, well let's go. I'll give you a ride."

The neighbor was all excited, so off they went onto the lake and got in Dad's plane. It was a nice clear, cold, sunny day. Dad warmed up the plane, revved it up and off they went. He took the neighbor low over the trees, did a few dives, a couple of spins, flew upside down, anything to impress this friend of his on his first plane ride with Dad.

After landing the plane, the poor guy looked pretty sick. They both went back into the Trading Post, and had a drink. After Dad was done with his drink, he decided it was time to head home while he still had light. He turned to his friend, who lived close to us, and asked him if he wanted a lift home. The poor guy was still a bit green, and holding on to the bar for dear life. Even after his drink. But he turned to Dad and said, "No way! Never again, I thought you were trying to kill me!" The guy was still holding onto the bar, with a tight grip, and still shakey when Dad left to come home.

After that ride, Dad saw him quite a few times on his visit to the Trading Post. And never again did the friend ask for a ride again.

When we were kids, he would take us up, and do the same. Dive the house, make quick swoops down, which always made us feel like we were loosing our stomachs. And we would scream so loud! When we came in from our rides, Mom would always tell us that she could hear our screams all the way in the house.

Scream as we might, we were always ready to go up again when he asked if we wanted to go for a ride.

*As recalled by DAN GIORDANO*

# Quick, Shut the Door

WE HAD AN OLD ALUMINUM SLED. And many times we would take it over the hill and spend many hours sliding down the hill, and hauling it back up and go at it again. It held 6 or 7 of us at one time, and the older kids would go with us. They did the dragging of the sled, while the younger ones climbed back up the hill. When we got home, we would put the sled out by the side of the house.

One particular time, the boys had used it to haul wood for the house, and after unloading it close to the door, they just left it in front of the door.

The next morning, Blackie, our dog, was out side. We could hear him barking, and wondered what was out there. Mom went to the door and pulled the curtain back to see what he was up to,

She was surprised to see he had agitated a moose. The moose had had enough of his barking, and nipping at her feet, and turned to chase him off.

Blackie only knew of one thing to do, head for the house and safety. So here was Blackie running for the house and the moose, not far behind him. Seeing all this Mom was in a quandary as to what to do. She called to one of my brothers and told him when she said, "Open the door" open it and shut it just as quick as he could.

My brother took his position at the door, Mom yelled "Open the door", my brother did, and in ran Blackie. I think my brother almost got the dogs tail, he shut the door so quick. Luckily, the moose tripped on the sled that my brothers had left in front of the door. Mom said another inch or so, and he would have shut the door on the moose's nose!

Blackie was very good at finding moose, and getting them so riled up that they would chase him. He would always head full speed for the house, and safety.

*MARY HALPIN*

# Iditarod

HAVING THE IDITAROD RACE run in Willow was a big surprise for me. When I told people I lived in Willow, the usual response was, "Where's Willow?" It was generally not on any maps. It is nice for me to see the maps now showing Willow, now.

In Willow, at first, very few people had dog teams, and those that did, had them for transportation, not racing.

My first dog team ride was not really planned. My son and I had walked up Hatcher Pass to visit a friend. She was a good cook, and had invited us for lunch. We had stayed and enjoyed her cooking, and the conversation. Being winter, we knew we had to leave in time to make it back home before dark, as in the winter, darkness fell early- -usually about 4 p.m. or so.

As we stepped out her door for our trip home, we spotted a moose down the road. Not wanting to encounter this moose, we asked her next door neighbor for a ride home. He had a truck, but no gas. But he did offer us a ride home in with his dog team. Hitching up the team, I was surprised to see the sled. It was an ochio, an army sled. Not the usual sled used by dog mushers. By now I was feeling a little bit dubious of this ride home. But between this, or the moose—some choice.

His dogs were of mixed breeds, and ready for the trip. I cautiously got in the sled. I sat in the middle on blankets, my son knelt behind me. Our neighbor was in front and yelled "Mush!" The dogs took off smoothly along till we rounded a corner. Sure enough, there was that moose. She was unwilling to leave the road, as hard, high snow berms lined the road sides. The dogs now stepped up their pace, and so did the moose. She ran faster, and faster. The ochio started whipping behind the dogs. My son was told to drag his feet, to act as a brake. The neighbor was yelling at his dogs to "whoa". I held onto the sides of the ochio, skinning my knuckles as it whipped side to side. Finally the moose, in desperation, jumped over the berm, and left the road and disappeared.

The dogs sped on, not even breaking their stride. I believe, if you could have clocked this team, that they surely must have been doing at least 60 mph! But we did make it home. Catching my breath, and making sure my son was okay, I was barely able to say thank you for our ride.

Mr. Nelson, on the south side of Willow, raised and sold dogs. It was his team that gave me my second ride. His team played the reindeer that pulled Santa's Sleigh, as I had told in an earlier story.

Earl Norris, another infamous name in the Iditarod history. Moved out to Willow, He owned the Howling Dog Farm and started out in Anchorage. He invited other mushers to stay and train at his farm.

Willow now hosts many mushers who enter the Iditarod

Race. Having the Iditarod restart in Willow is a rare occasion. It is only held in Willow, when there is lack of snow in Wasilla.

Four-Mile Road, where we lived in Willow, now have at least four residents that now have dog teams. Most own over 100 dogs, and you could always tell when it was time for feeding of the dogs. If you could imagine the noise that 300 dogs could make, howling and barking, while waiting for their meal.

When we moved to Palmer, many people would ask why we moved. Jokingly, I said, "I think Willow has gone to the dogs!"

*"MOM" GIORDANO*

# More Dogs

WHEN MY NEXT TO THE YOUNGEST SISTER got married, they moved 3 miles back in the woods. They would have to cross Deception Creek, and walk a cart path back to their cabin. In the summer, they walked across a cable bridge, now they were tricky.

A cable bridge, has two cables leading from one side of the creek to the other, usually about 10 feet or so above the water. It then had cables running down to another set of cables. Then they would take slat of board to make the walk way. But being cable, they sure swayed a lot.

In the winter they had a dog team for the ride out. Having children in school, they would come out with the dog team, early enough to stop at grandma's house to warm up, and then walk the rest of the way to the bus stop, which was only a half-mile from grandma's house.

She would pull in with the team, get them tethered down, and come in for a visit with Mom and to warm up. She could handle a team with no trouble. But then she was the wood cutter, cabinet maker of their household. Her husband worked construction during the summer, and winter was a time for resting. He did help her in the winter, though, when it came time to haul water, and chop wood.

One day her husband decided he needed something from Willow, and took the team out to our house. The next thing we know, here comes their team with no rider. They knew exactly where to go. They pulled into our yard, went right to where my sister would have tethered them, if she had been there.

Shortly after, here comes her husband, madder that a wet hen. When we asked what had happened he told us that he had hit a snow-covered stump, knocking him off the back runners of the sled. He called for them to "whoa", but the dogs just kept going. After all, they knew the trail well enough that they didn't need any one to tell them what was expected.

They lived back in the woods for quite a few years. Had many dealings with bears, and moose. Now me, I would have said, "No Thanks." I called myself the most typically homesteader's wife, Give me hot and cold running water, a flip of the switch for lights, a good furnace for heat, and of course my TV., and I was a happy camper.

I give my sister plenty of credit, even today she works more like a man. She has made Mom tables, put up wood shelves, and her latest was a beautiful replica of a hutch.

*MARY HALPIN*

# Another School Year

LIVING IN WILLOW, shopping for school clothes was done by Sears and Roebuck (now, just Sears) catalog. She would flip through the book and pick out what we had to have- 3 pair of jeans for each of the boys, 3 lined flannel corduroy pants for the girls, because you could get them in different colors, turtlenecks for the girls, flannel shirts for the boys—the usual array of socks, underwear (including long johns), for all. My oldest sister had more leniency, after all she was in high school, and a lot more pressure from her peers came her way.

She did pick out 2 dresses for us girls, that we could choose from, 1 considered them bad to worse!! But with such a huge family, you just went along with what Mom said.

If we wanted anything special, we had to earn moneys our self. Now, there wasn't many jobs for children then. I went to work at the Willow Trading Post doing odd jobs, cleaning, working in the kitchen arranging and cleaning the pantry and cupboards. My sisters and I also picked berries by the gallons for the Trading Post, as they made pies and cakes themselves.

Then when my oldest sister started having babies, so we became babysitters, which helped add to our money making.

I was so proud, at the age of 12, I bought my first dress that I got to pick on my own. It was a sleeveless A-line dress in a pretty shade of green. I just loved it, but then came time for its first washing—Tragedy—not knowing much of laundry, I put bleach in the water (after I put the dress in) no one told me I had to put bleach in first and mix it up so it wouldn't ruin the dress. Yep, when I went back to hand wash my dress and hang it up to dry-I now had a green and white spotted dress!! I learned real fast the value of reading labels!

*MARY HALPIN*

Willow's first basketball team. Mary's brother is on the far right.

# Moose in the Wood Lot

ONE THING ABOUT CLEARING land around your house, it meant for at least the first few years, firewood wouldn't be to hard to get to.

It was the 3 older boys job to keep our house ready with firewood. In the summer, you try to stock up on firewood, but eventually you had to cut more. This one winter we had quite a bit of snow, well over 6', moose just didn't like moving around much, so they headed to where food was readily available, which meant our front yard!

As the boys headed out to cut the wood, they came face to face with a huge mamma moose-and she wasn't going to go away. They tried everything from yelling, throwing snowballs, you name it they tried it. Mom in the meantime had come out with our movie camera and was filming this comical event.

But fun was fun, the boys still had to cut wood, and whenever they got to close to the trees to be cut, this moose would charge at them, and our crazy dog! My oldest brother suggested getting out the 22 rifle, Mom agreed to let him give it a try, so he shot a branch down, and it landed on the back of this ornery moose, no good, she just lowered her head and came at all of them, you could tell by the film, even Mom was getting out of harms way.

Well, after that, the boys got a reprieve from cutting wood. My Mom told them we had enough wood for a day or so, and maybe she would be gone by morning. Now the boys wanted ole' mamma moose to hang around for awhile, but when we woke up in the morning to see if our unexpected guest was still around, she had wandered off to a quieter dining area. Which meant it was time for the boys to get out the axes and chainsaws and start cutting wood.

*MARY HALPIN*

# Campfire Dinner

HAVING NINE CHILDREN to entertain, was always a challenge for Mom. She started out in Massachusetts, as a den mother for my brothers boy scouts, brownie leader for us girls, and as we grew older, the a girl scout leader.

Moving to Alaska didn't change much for her in that direction. She started brownies again in Willow, a different situation from Mass., in Willow, sometimes the parents didn't come to pick up their children, either because of distance, or bad roads, so a lot of times a few girls spent the night. When we got older, it was girl scouts again. Being older, she would take us camping. We still had badges to earn, and we all worked hard at earning them.

On the camping trips she would teach us how to live off the land. Dandelions made a good source of iron, you would cook them just like you would any other vegetable, no, I never found them to tasty. Then there were young sprouts of fireweed, one of Alaska's flowers that grew abundantly. The young sprouts were good to use in salad's, or if you had nothing else, just make a salad of them.

The best thing she ever taught us, though, was how to

make a meal without using a pan. You take one potato, diced, one small onion, chopped, and hamburger made into small meat balls. Season with salt and pepper, or garlic, if you had some. Then you would wrap all these ingredients in foil, set it in the campfire for about an hour. It's a real tasty, and economical meal, when out in the woods.

When I babysat for my oldest sister, the kids were always glad I was coming. They knew that night, we would have a campfire dinner, and get to play outside while it was cooking.

I would help each one make their own. I would dice up the potatoes and onion, they would have to make their own meat balls. I let
them season their own meal, and wrap the foil. I would put each one in the campfire, telling them to keep an eye on which was theirs. Then we would play hide and seek, or tag, or just sit around the fire and tell stories. I had each one tell a story.

I never thought much of those occasions, I just figured it was an easy meal, no dishes, and kept them entertained. But years later, when the oldest boy had married, I came for a visit. He told me the best memory he had of my babysitting was they knew they were having campfire dinner. He said all the kids loved it because they knew they could fix their own dinner, have a picnic, and play lots of games outside till it was bedtime.

*MARY HALPIN*

# Witch of Willow

FOR 25 YEARS, I was known as the Witch of Willow. It started in 1959, when Bob and Betty Douglas, owners of the Willow Trading Post, decided to have a Halloween party. Costume contest and all.

Do you remember poodle skirts? Huge circular skirts with a poodle on it. Well, my oldest daughter had one, without a poodle. An ideal witches cape. I wore one of my long black dresses with the skirt as my cape, and all I needed was hat. My hair was long and streaked with gray, so I didn't need a wig. When we arrived at the party, I made Dan go in first. I had always worn my hair in a braid, and wrapped around my head, so I knew they wouldn't recognize me with my hair down. I kept them all guessing for awhile, then came the contest. I was so excited, I had won best costume for women. The prize was $5!

I had so much fun, that I decided to go to the school and entertain the kids. My oldest daughter said, "Mother, if you do, I'll never speak to you again!" Well—I had to see.

That year and every year after I went to school and gave

away candy, and read spooky tales. When the kids got rowdy, I would tell them if they weren't good I'd change them into a toad. It seemed to work.

Then they decided to start a Halloween Carnival at the school to keep the kids off the streets. Then the old witch came to the carnival and sold apple cider, using a huge kettle as a cauldron.

One year Dad's construction kept him in Soldotna during Halloween. I had gone down to stay with him. I went to the local school there and asked if they would like to have a witch come to visit. They were more than glad to have the extra entertainment. Again I gave away candy, told spooky stories, and threatened to turn them into toads if they weren't good little boys and girls.

Now in Soldotna, in a strange school, it was hard telling who was more scared? Me, or the kids. Soldotna had 300 kids in their school—Willow only had 60 to 80. I bought a lot of candy for that school. I had to go from store to store, at that time Soldotna wasn't very big, town wise. When I retired, I asked one of my younger daughters to take over for me. Being she had kids in Willow school, she accepted. She did it once and said, "Never again."

Now, Mary, on the other hand, dressed up for all occasions for the dialysis centers. A witch at Halloween, cupid at valentines day, Santa's "Lil" Elf at Christmas, etc. She even managed to make an outfit for the New Years Baby. She handed out candy, and went to different wards in the hospital where she dialysed. She said the most favorite ward in Swedish Hospital, in Seattle was the cancer ward. Beings they had cancer, and a lot of bone marrow transplants were done there, they had very low immune systems. So it was hard to keep up sterile conditions, and still allow outside visitors. They did their best to keep the kids spirits up, but didn't have too much entertainment for them. Oh, they had a lady come around at a specific time of day to read stories, or play games with the children. But she said when the witch showed up with a pumpkin full of candy, there eyes really lit up.

*"MOM" GIORDANO*

Mary at Alaska Kidney Center—1995

# What Was That?

AFTER BUYING HIS PLANE, he often flew to work in it. He did love to fly, so besides transportation to work, it gave him a reason to take the plane up (as if he needed one). I did worry about his flying to work when the weather looked marginal.

I remember one winter say, it looked like it might snow. I mentioned this to him as he was warming up the plane. He said if it snowed to come and get me. They were working on a road in the Talkeetna area, so I could drive up and get him. I was still new at driving, so I kept close to home.

By the afternoon we had a full blown snow storm, and visibility was very marginal. So I prepared supper and drove up the highway towards Talkeetna to pick up Dan. Sure he wouldn't try flying in this weather.

Driving north, even I had a hard time seeing the road. I also was keeping one eye out for Dad as I realized he would have to fly the highway to find his way home. I kept telling myself (trying to convince myself) that he wouldn't be crazy enough to try flying home in this kind of weather. He had flown home once in a wild wind storm, so bad that everything that was loose inside the plane, was hitting him and dropping to the floor. He had told me not to come get him that time. My son took me, as he too was worried about Dan's ability to fly in that hard of wind. That time we met him on the Depot road, whistling, and swinging his lunch pale as he started to walk home. He hadn't dared to try landing on our little airport in back on the cabin, so he landed on the Willow airstrip.

Still keeping a watchful eye, and hoping he hadn't decided to try flying home from Talkeetna, I suddenly saw a set of wheels that were inches from the car, I could have probably reached out and touched them!! Sure enough, that was Dan. I couldn't believe it. I found a turn around and headed back home. Thinking how crazy he was, even I had no business being on these roads, let alone an airplane flying in this weather.

I drove home fuming and fussing all the way home about this idiot of a husband. By the time I got home I had a full head of steam, and he got both barrels when I got there. He just let me vent off my steam, laughed, and said, "You get to excited, I had everything under control."

There were a few other incidents over the years and his usual answer was not to worry- he knew what he was doing and had everything under control. He sure made our lives interesting to say the least.

*"MOM" GIORDANO*

# Being in Style

GROWING UP IN WILLOW, and getting to an age where being in style with your friends was real important.

Mom had a rule, we girls had to get on a chair on our knees, and if our skirt or dress hemline met the chair, we could wear it. Mini skirts were just coming into style, but style meant nothing to Mom. Of course we left the house with a regular length skirt (Mom's version) but by the time we got to school, a couple turns of the waist band put us right in style with the other girls.

Winter didn't make much difference in keeping in style— if it was 20 below, we still wore our skirts short, nylons and "white" tennis shoes. It helped having a brother-in-law that owned the school bus company, and made a point of coming up to the house to pick us up. Of course we had to run the whole route with him, but we didn't mind. We were warm, and in style!!

The girls had to a lot of work during summer, to supplement our school wardrobe, as Mom ordered what she thought we should have, being practical, and economical. But we always managed to make enough (especially since my sister and her husband bowled once a week and we got to baby sit for them.) to buy a dress we liked, or a pair of shoes we liked.

Dad was also into the practicality of life. In Palmer, we had a store called "Johnny' Surplus." It had a little bit of everything, kitchen appliances, utensils, most anything to fix up a home. Traps, trapping gear, you name it he probably had it somewhere. This one day, Dad stopped in just out of boredom, and he just happened to find a pair of wedge nursing shoes-and they were just 50 cents! He bought the shoes and brought them home, all 3 of us girls just looked at them in horror, wondering who was going to get the pleasure of owning these shoes. I was very lucky, only being the size of a 6 year old, but being 13, they were to big for me. I can't remember who got to claim those shoes. But it sure caused a commotion for awhile over those shoes.

Now, looking at shoes in the stores, I see wedge shoes all the time. I even own a couple pair myself! Who would have know that in 1960s we were already in style, and just didn't know it!
When my youngest sister and I rented an apartment in Anchorage, many years later. We decided to get wild and wear a miniskirt, nylons and white tennis shoes down to a local bar. We no sooner got out the door, and the thought of looking sharp and being in style went right out the window. We quickly went back in the apartment and put on our jeans and boots!!

*MARY HALPIN*

# *Bologna or Hot Dog*

I HAD FORGOTTEN THIS particular past incident. Just the other day I decided to fix lunch for us all. Dad, Mom, and myself. We were going to have hotdogs. Dad and Mom wanted theirs cooked, with mustard and relish. I always ate mine raw, and sliced length wise, made into a sandwich.

After getting lunch ready, and setting it on the table, we started to eat. Dad asked me what was I having. I told him I was having a bologna sandwich. Well, Mom just started laughing, while Dad looked at me like I was crazy.

I started to tell him what was so funny. When we were children, after Mom learned how to drive, we would go shopping once a week in Anchorage. Mom would buy extra, so on the way home we could stop at the Eagle River Campground and have a picnic lunch. She bought a package of hotdogs, potato chips, soda, and all the trimmings. She also bought a package of bologna for me because I told her I didn't like hotdogs.

One day, after shopping, we went to the campground

as usual. She had bought my package of bologna for me as always. But as she was preparing the hotdogs, she was trying to explain to me that hotdogs and bologna were basically the same thing. One was round, and one was flat. Of course, at the age of 12 I knew that a hotdog was a hotdog, and bologna was bologna. And I insisted that I didn't like hotdogs, and she was just trying to trick me.

After listening to me go on about the subject, she said we could solve the question real easy. She said, "I'll cut up a hotdog, not cooked, and I'll cut up a piece of bologna. You close your eyes, and I'll give you a piece of each, and you tell me which is a hotdog and which bologna." Well, I was game for that, I'd prove to her that I really didn't like hotdogs.

She put a blindfold on me, and gave me a piece of meat, I proudly told her that it was a piece of bologna. Then she gave me the second piece of meat, and I told her that it was also bologna, and she was trying to confuse me. She then took off the blindfold, and gave me a piece of bologna to taste, which I did, then she gave me a piece of hotdog- -I hesitated, but did taste it. Mmmm, could I have been wrong all this time?

From then on, she only bought hotdogs, and I ate them raw in a bun with onion. Later on I started to slice them thin enough length ways and made hotdog sandwiches.

So to this day, whenever hotdogs are brought up, that's the first thing that comes to mind, and we still get a laugh out of it.

Actually, Mom is a fanatic on hotdogs. When she came down to help me through one of my kidney transplants in Seattle, and I was released from the hospital, but had to stay close to the hospital, we would go out for a drive, or go have lunch. Heading back home if she spotted a hotdog stand, we had to stop, I think in that one month's time, she knew every hotdog stand within a mile of the hospital!!

*MARY HALPIN*

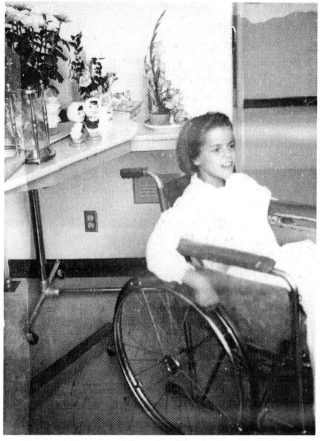

Mary age 11.

# Where's the Beef

WHEN YOU MOVE out and live in the sticks, you become many things. Cook, nurse, mechanic, janitor, etc. What ever was needed to done, you just got in and did it.

The first moose I had to "butcher" (and butcher it I did), it was a real task. One quarter of a moose took up our whole table and then some. I didn't know anything about cutting across the grain, or follow a muscle structure-I just hacked it up—we sure had a lot of hamburger off that one.

As time went by, I got pretty good at getting nice steaks, and roasts off one of those magnificent animal. I found cutting with the grain, your meat was stringy, very chewy! It was sure nice having a little variety in our meats, instead of hamburger. My favorite part of the moose, though, was the liver. I think I was the only one that enjoyed it. Many neighbors also brought me the liver from their moose, also, but I never got tired of liver.

In the early days of homesteading you could hunt from the road. So Dan always carried his 30-30 rifle with him. You could shoot a moose then for each member of your family, whew! 11 moose a year, we could feed the whole community! But there were times when a moose would just be so easy to shoot, and close to the road, you just couldn't resist.

This particular occasion Dan and I were coming back from town, and there were two moose standing side by side, so Dan stopped and shot at the first moose. It didn't drop, and Dan said, darn (sounds better than the actual word) I missed it. It took off like a shot, but low and behold, the one on the other side fell.

Apparently, when he shot, the bullet went through the "beard" on the first moose, and hit the second one in the neck in the jugular vein!

Yes, Dan had to take me home, then go back with the boys and clean the moose and bring it home—no, I didn't get off easy, for when they brought the moose in, I got the pleasure of butchering it up, and wrapping the meat for later use. Being winter, we could leave the meat out in the meat house till we were ready for more meat, thank heavens!!

*"MOM" GIORDANO*

# Ice Fishing

WINTER WAS NEVER one of my most favorite times of the year when I got older. I was never athletic, didn't care about snow machines, skiing or any of those things.

When I got married, my husband was quite the opposite. Trapping, hunting, fishing, snow machines, if it had anything to do with the great outdoors, he was ready!

He was in the army out of Fort Richardson. And he had 2 years of "rough" duty. He was sent to Seward to run charter boats for the army and air force personnel. His boat was considered the best to go out on, cause people always caught fish- no matter if they had fished before or not.

But his favorite fishing was in the winter, when we would go down to Grouse Lake, outside of Seward, and do some ice fishing. We would head out the night before to get an early start the next day. We would go with my sister and her husband. We'd stay in our vehicles that night, get up and go have breakfast and then on to the lake for some fishing.

He would chop a hole in the lake, and drop his line in.

Sometimes it was hard to see what you were fishing for, so out came the army blankets, They would cover themselves up over the hole, and it was just like daylight in the water, and you could see the fish swim by and just about pick which one you wanted.

You noticed I said they, being the avid winter person, I always chose to stay and keep the car warm. Watching from the car was always fun. You could see all the different antics fishermen had for catching fish.

Tom, my husband, always seemed to start a trend for catching fish. One year it was the blanket trick, it caught on quite well, and from the car Grouse Lake looked like a battle field —- covered bodies every where. Then one year, he painted his lure white, next thing you know people are coming up to him offering him money to paint their lures. No, he never charged them.

The last year I can remember going to Seward to fish, we had forgotten to get fishing licenses. But we went fishing anyway. My nephew was the only one with a license.

That year a game warden was making his rounds on the lake to see who had licenses. So grabbing our blankets and fishing paraphernalia, we headed off the lake to go into Seward and get our licenses. Upon our return, the game warden had already left. But at least we were legal then.

The funniest time I can remember about our ice fishing trips, was when Tom lost track of his fish.

Sitting in my usual place, keeping the car warm, I was watching every one fish. People under blankets, when they would get a fish, they would just pop out from under their blanket and throw the fish on the ice next to them. Tom included.

After catching a few fish, Tom decided it was time to count his catch. I had been watching from the car, and as Tom would catch a fish and toss it on the lake, an eagle would swoop down and take it up to his tree and proceed to eat. This went on for about 3 times, of this eagle feasting on Tom's fish. So it was quite a site to watch from the car, as Tom went from fishermen to fishermen and ask them if they saw who took his fish. They all replied that they hadn't seen anything.

Tom went back under his blanket to fishing. He had put two fish up on the lake, and had a third ready. About the time he came out from under his blanket, the eagle also chose to swoop down and nab some more lunch. I don't know who was more startled, Tom at seeing the eagle, or the eagle coming face to face with an army blanket being tossed in his direction.

*MARY HALPIN*

# Watch Out! Mom's Driving

ALL MY MEMORIES are of Willow. Yes, I shopped in Palmer, Anchorage and Wasilla. But Willow was home.

I found out after short time that one must learn to drive to be able to do anything. I had to haul water, get my mail at the post office, six miles away. And do my grocery shopping.

Many times I walked to the post office and back home. But I had to wait until Dad got home from work for water and grocery shopping. I had to learn to drive.

I had watched Dad and his driving and the questions were easy if you used common sense.

Now the hard part. Thank goodness we had an automatic drive car. I took the car into the back field to get the feel of it. Then I drove up and down 4-mile Road. Hatcher Pass was still a gravel road and I drove two or three miles down it. Now I was driving Hatcher Pass, going to the post office to pick up my mail. Also helped the boys haul water from Willow Creek.

Sternly, Dad said, "If your going to drive on these roads, you need a license". One day my new son-in-law came and said, "C'mon, Dad says you got to get your license today". Bravely I got into his car and we headed for Palmer. Halfway there he stopped and told me to take the wheel. So, I drove to Palmer.

But when he got out and the officer got in, I was scared stiff, and so nervous. I drove around the block and remembered my daughter had parked too far from the curb. I wanted to make sure I was closer. I heard the officer suck in his breath as I slid past a fire hydrant and came to a halt at a legal distance from the hydrant.

I told the officer I would only drive in Willow. He said he thought I was really nervous, but I had done well. He signed the license and looked me straight in the eye and said, "Go home and kill them all!"

That same week Dad bought me a New Yorker, Take it to Anchorage Monday and get heavier tires on it. Anchorage? Me? He said, "No problem, its on 5th Avenue." I drove to Anchorage that day and every week after that. I followed Dad to several of his construction jobs during the summer. We got to see Homer, Soldotna, Kenai, Seward, Delta Junction, Circle Hot Springs, and even Fairbanks.

Yes, I'm still driving today, at the age of 80!!

*"MOM" GIORDANO*

Dan on our trip to Talkeetna with no road.

# Is That Your Dog?

ONE OF MY BROTHERS had decided to surprise Dad and Mom with a visit. He decided to hitchhike from Anchorage out to Willow.

As he was hiking along, he could hear some rustling in the bushes along side of where he was walking. Not being able to see what was there, he was getting a bit nervous. After all this was Alaska and in the early 60s there were quite a few bear and moose around. Just as he decided he'd had enough, and whatever it was, was about to come through the bushes, he raised his leg to kick whatever was there. Much to his surprise, it was a goat.

He continued to hitchhike home, but this goat just kept following him. He kept trying to chase it off, but to no avail. He would chase it and it would run off a short distance, and as soon as my brother continued on his way, the goat would just start to follow him again.

We had a neighbor that just happened to be heading home at that time. He apparently had stopped to have a few drinks before going home. But he recognized my brother, and stopped to ask if he wanted a lift. My brother accepted gladly, if anything to get rid of his traveling companion.

Realizing that the goat was still there, he again, tried to chase this crazy goat away. He no sooner opened the door to accept the ride, when his "traveling companion" came out of no where and jumped into the car also.

Having had a few drinks on his way home, the neighbor didn't seem to take notice that a goat had jumped in his car. All he asked my brother was, "Is that your dog?" To this day, I don't know if the neighbor ever realized that what he thought was a dog, actually was a goat!

*MARY HALPIN*

# Dan Jr. and the Beaver

WINTER WAS DAD'S favorite time of the year. Not because he like the cold, but it was the only time he had to call his own. He worked in road construction till the weather shut down the roadwork.

One thing he really enjoyed was taking his plane up, either to go hunting, or trapping, or just taking Mom down to the Willow Trading Post. Being the only restaurant, bar, liquor store, etc.—it was considered a local watering hole!!

One day he decided it was time to check his trap line. He took my older brother with him, and off they went to see how well they had done in trapping some beaver.

Upon landing and going to one of the beaver traps, they noticed that one beaver was very much alive. So instead of killing the beaver, they decided they would bring it home. They wrapped the beaver in a coat. My brother got the honor of holding this beaver on the flight home, after all Dad had to fly the plane!

My brother had a death grip on this beaver, and all the

way home Dad kept saying. "Don't let go son, don't let go!" They made it home with this live beaver, showed it off to all of us kids, then came the problem of where they were going to keep this cute little beaver.

My brother and his wife lived across the street from us, and their house had a nice bathroom- with a nice tub— just the right size for our new guest. So they put the beaver in the tub.

Now, to say my sister-in-law was impressed would not be very truthful. Aside from the fact that this was a wild animal in her bathroom, it didn't help much when she went in to the bathroom and this creature would hiss at her the whole time she was there.

As a child, I thought this was exciting—looking back at it now, I could just picture my brother holding on to this beaver in a plane, torn between trusting Dad to get them home with this live animal inside of that small plane, and hoping like crazy that he didn't lose his grip on the beaver. I don't know which one was crazier, Dad or my brother! Or my sister-in-law allowing the beaver to occupy their bathroom.

I'm not sure I would have been as agreeable as she was. But as a child, I thought it was pretty neat, because we were allowed to go see it.

*AS TOLD BY DAN GIORDANO*

# Let's Dance

IN THE LAST FEW years we've been going down to Dawson City for our anniversary. Dad, Mary and I would take off and go over the Taylor Highway, nicknamed the Top Of The World Highway, because it ran the mountain tops all the way until you came to the Yukon, and there you took a short ferry ride (about 15 minutes) to the city.

The highlight of our trip was going to Diamond Tooth Gertie, she performed a gold rush style dancing and singing revue as done in the old gold rush days in Dawson. We had met her in our first trip, so it was like going to see an old friend. Her shows were funny, she did three shows a night, and she would always do a number where she would get some volunteers from the audience to help her out, as she put it.

On our 57th anniversary, I had asked the musicians to sing and play "our" song, "It Had To Be You." She was so nice, Diamond Tooth Gertie came out and announced it over the microphone, and she sang our song.

Later she came over and talked to me. Dad was playing

cards then. Later at the 10 p.m. show, Dad came to join me at the table. She went on with her show. She said she had always had a fantasy where she danced with two men at one time. Going out into the audience, she grabbed one guy named Charlie, as she hauled him toward the stage she turned to Dan and said, "C'mon Danny." I never saw a man jump out of a chair so fast- and one that didn't dance at that. She said they were going to sing, Dan said, "I don't sing." She began to sing, telling Charlie and Dan to repeat after her. Charlie did fine, but Dan just repeated again, "I don't sing!" On her last part of the song, she stopped to turn to Charlie, who sang, but when she turned to Dan she said, "I know, I know, you don't sing!" finally they got to the dancing part. She turned again to Charlie, who did his part, but when she got to Dan, well his "I don't want to!" just brought the down the house!! A lot of people came over and introduced themselves, asked about our secret to a long marriage, and even took pictures of us together.

*"MOM" GIORDANO*

Our 56th Wedding Anniversary.

Dan and Mom in Dawson City.

# Redwing Boots

ONE OF THE THINGS that Mom wanted upon our arrival in Alaska, was a pair of red wing boots. She was afraid of snakes, and not knowing if there were any in Alaska, she figured she would be safe helping to clear the land with a pair of high-top boots.

Living in Massachusetts, there were always snakes. One of my brothers actually had a collection of snakes preserved in alcohol for a school project.

After arriving in Alaska, Dad bought her the Red Wings she wanted, and boy did we have to be careful after that! If we got to close to her new boots she would say, "Watch out for my new boots!" She was one proud lady having her own Red Wings.

One day her and Dad were going to town. We were already at the creek fishing. They stopped by to let us know where they were going and what we needed to do before they got home. Of course there were a lot of other people fishing there also, and upon seeing all those salmon in the creek, Mom got excited. So her and Dad went up to our little hardware store, picked up

70

some fishing gear and came back to try their hand at salmon fishing.

Mom was getting frustrated though, because if just seemed that the fish were always on the opposite side of the creek! The next thing we see is our Mom in the middle of the creek, dressed in a nice dress, earrings, necklace (and her Red Wings) having the time of her life! She was finally catching fish and she was excited.

Now we kids were watching all this going on, and just laughing at the sight of Mom in the middle of the creek, dressed for town, and of all things—in her new boots.

We called out to her, "Mom. Your getting your new boots wet!" She turned and called back, "Yep! But I'm catching fish!"

Now her Red Wings were truly broke in, and we didn't have to worry anymore about getting to close to her "new" Red Wings!!

*MARY HALPIN*

# One That Didn't Get Away

OUR FIRST SUMMER in Alaska, Dad got to do some fishing. He hadn't had time yet to find work because he was building our cabin, and getting us set up for the winter.

We lived between two creeks. Willow Creek was about a half mile or so from our house in one direction, and Deception Creek was about the same distance in the other direction. So fishing was a main source of entertainment for all of us, Dad included.

Mom had a rule in the house, if you catch it, you clean it. Of course we younger ones got out of that, after all we were to young to handle a knife. That really upset us girls, you can be sure.

One day, Dad decided to take a break from all the work he had been doing and went fishing. So off he went over the hill to Willow Creek and try fishing before dinner time. I think it was Willow Creek, you have to remember, I was only 9 then, now I'm 49!

The king salmon were running then. The name fit them

perfect, they were the biggest of all salmon, and I found it fascinating to watch these majestic fish swim around.

Dad hadn't been gone to long, and we were waiting for him to return. Then we saw him coming up over the hill so we ran to meet him. He had caught a fish, and was it ever big. My Dad is probably 5' 5", and he had this fish slung over his shoulder. This fish reached from his shoulders, and the tail was dragging on the ground. Being we were small children, this fish sure looked big to us!!

Mom was shocked to see such a huge fish, and proceeded to clean it. We had fish for dinner, and then Mom canned the rest.

I did find out, that not just little kids got out of cleaning their catch. Dad's have special privileges, too!!

*MARY HALPIN*

# Close Calls


DAN FLEW HIS AERONICA CHAMP to work, trapping, or just sight seeing. His boss, children and I often worried about this man who thought he was invincible when he was in his plane.

One day his boss called to him after he parked his plane and asked, " Did you come in over that wire, or under it?" Dan looked up and said, "What wire?" Dan either didn't see the wire or he was just giving the boss a bad time because he knew the boss always worried about him and his antics.

In the winter, your plane has to have plenty of time to warm up before take off. One particular night, Dan was getting ready to head home with his plane, he was tired (and impatient) so when he started the plane, he didn't want to wait for the plane to warm up. So off he went. When he got airborne, shortly after the engine stalled. After a few dives, he did manage to get it started without any problems. When he got home he didn't mention anything of his close call to me.

The next night, he went to start his plane to let it warm

up, when he noticed a note on the windshield of his plane. He had figured he had got away with his stupid stunt and no one had seen what happened when he took off the other night without warming his plane.

The note was a simple one and unsigned. It simply said, "I'm like a woman, I need to be warm to be good!" He didn't live that one down for awhile.

I knew of some of his close calls, but then there were some he never talked about, mainly not to let me worry, but also because were dumb things he had done, and didn't want anyone to know.

"MOM" GIORDANO

# *Mom's First Mother's Day*

IN AN EARLIER STORY, my Mom wrote about the different gifts she got from her "darling" children, and how she thought each one was trying to outdo the other in the type of gifts they gave her. It brought back a memory I had of Mom's first Mother's Day in Alaska.

Dad had to clear 20 acres of land to keep in line of earning our homestead deed. Plus it had to be seeded. It just so happened that he found a good buy on an old D-7 cat. It was in good enough shape to do the work he had to do. So he made the deal with the fellow that was selling this piece of equipment.

Now came the problem of trying to explain to Mom why he decided to buy the equipment after she had said it wasn't a good idea because of their financial situation. She was looking at the family side of money, food, clothing, and keeping us on track. Dad, of course, was looking at the task he had in front of him of clearing 20 acres.

Now, being the romantic(?) person that Dad was, and keeping in line with it being close to Mother's Day, he went to the fellow that he had bought the D-7 from and told him he would buy the piece of equipment, but he had to deliver it on Mother's Day with a banner on it saying "HAPPY MOTHER'S DAY!"

To say Mom was excited, and thrilled by this most fabulous gift any woman could ever receive could hardly define her true feelings on this particular present.

But we kids sure enjoyed it, each one got a chance to ride it. My oldest sister actually got to run it, come to think of it, my Dad even put my little brother on it for him to work it.

I got reminded of it many years later, after I was married. My husband bought me a 270 rifle. Being only 4'6", it was quite a heavy rifle, Not to worry, for Tom had the answer to my problem. He simply said he had that covered, he would be nice and use it for me!!

*MARY HALPIN*

# The Party's Over

THE OTHER DAY DAD said we had to go to the concrete place and order a truck load of cement for our back yard. We were making a cement pad for our picnic table so it would be easier to mow the grass without having to move the table every time.

Upon arriving at the concrete plant, my Dad got to talking to the guy taking our order. He asked if his Dad still ran the company or not. The man answered yes, and that his Dad still worked there part time just to keep himself occupied. The my Dad asked him if he wasn't the "little pissy-pants" that "helped" his Dad in the early years. The guy just laughed and said, "Yep! That was me!!"

Then Dad started to tell us of the time he and a couple of his friends came in to Wasilla to get a load of sand, cement mix, and blocks to build a foundation for a house. He told us that he had used the old Rio truck, by then made into a flat bed for hauling all these supplies back to Willow over the rough roads. They set blocks around the outside edges of the flat bed to hold the sand and cement bags in place for the ride home.

After getting everything loaded on the back of the truck, they decided to head for local bar and hoist a few drinks before the ride home. After having a "few" drinks, they decided it was time to head out. One of the friends wasn't ready to go, so he became obnoxious, not wanting to get in the truck, then threatening to jump out of the truck. Now Dad was getting a bit frustrated and tired of listening to the obnoxious neighbor, so he and the other friend just took the guy and put him on the top of the sand and cement, then cinched him down—just like you would a load of logs!!

Dad said it was later in the fall and a bit nippy, and all the way home the poor neighbor they had cinched down, was yelling, "I'm cold! Get me down from here! I'm cold!" But Dad just kept driving home.

I would just imagine after riding home all cinched up and freezing from riding on the back of that truck on those rough roads, that guy was surely sober by the time they got him back home!!

*RECALLED BY DAN GIORDANO*

# Fort Giordano

LIVING IN THE WILDERNESS, I call it that because that's just what it was—lots and lots of woods!

Anyway, as I started to say, living in the wilderness we children were left to find ways to have fun, and get out from Moms way as she cleaned and cooked.

When Dad had cleared the twenty acres, it left a lot of windrows—the object was to find a section of the windrow where the trees over lapped and made a hollow space. We would get in these hollows and make forts out of them.

We used stumps for chairs, and a table, or if we got lucky, one of the branches made an ideal bench or table. Then we would bring our lunch out their. For us as kids, this was really neat.

Then Mom would help us make a grocery store of our own. When she opened a can of veggies, she would open them upside down so when you put them on the shelf in your "new" store, they actually looked like the real thing. We had vegetables, soup, chili, whatever Mom had used for our dinners or lunch. When the jam or peanut butter was gone, or the powdered milk box was empty we added them to our store.

Now we had a fort, and a grocery store. We would work on these for days, and as kids we sure played a lot out there. Our forts were made close to the house, after all there were still moose and bear around.

Mom liked it because even though she enjoyed the peace and quiet, she still kept a watchful eye to make sure we were okay —I think she was just making sure we weren't out there fighting amongst each other!!

*MARY HALPIN*

# Flying the Traplines

ONCE CONSTRUCTION SEASON shut down for the winter, Dan had plenty of time now for relaxation. Naturally, his plane was top on his list for relaxing.

He had a few traplines out, one on top of Hatcher Pass, and another across the Big Susitna river.

One particular day he asked me to accompany him, of course it took a little coaxing as I wasn't that fond of flying. But I finally agreed to go along.

His trap line was approximately two miles long and it started from a small lake on top of Hatcher Pass. As we came in for the landing I was thinking how small it looked and was a bit nervous about landing, but I decided that he knew what he was doing.

I walked the line with him for about half of the trap line and grew tired from walking in the snow. So I decided that he should go on and I'd wait for him at this spot.

Sitting alone on a snow-covered mountain on a nice sunny day, I was enjoying experiencing a blessed quiet. With 9 children, that was an event I hardly got to enjoy. The longer I sat there, the more foolish I felt, and a bit nervous as well. Suppose a moose or a bear came by.

Or a wolf for that matter. After all, he trapped along a well used trail by animals. Why, anything could come by I thought. Then I got to looking around, and on the far off ridge were two wolves looking down on me. They never moved towards me, they were probably trying to figure out what this crazy woman was doing in the middle of nowhere and just sitting on a stump enjoying the scenery.

About that time Dan returned and we headed back to the lake and our plane. Getting in the plane, once again I thought this lake looked "real" small. Come to think of it, it looked smaller on the ground than in the air when I first got sight of it. But into the plane we climbed.

I looked at Dan rather nervously, and asked how we were to get off this lake? His simple reply was, "Don't worry, just relax." We got settled in the plane and Dan started warming up the plane for our trip home. Then he started revving up the engine full bore and when he released it we shot across that lake like a shot. We hit a bog and the plane bounced into the air, and we were air borne and flew home with no problems.

I flew many more times with him on top of Hatcher Pass, but never flew with him across the Big Sue. Crazy, huh? But at the same time it was exhilarating and I loved it.

*"MOM" GIORDANO*

Old miner's cabin.

Bible Camp at Giordano's homestead.

Willow's first school bus.